CW01213043

Auntie Says...
QUICK WISDOM
FOR GRADUATES

THE NEPHEW REVIEW

DENEAN BENNETT

CLAY BRIDGES
PRESS

Auntie Says:
Quick Wisdom for Graduates (The Nephew Review Edition)

Copyright © 2024 by Denean Bennett

Published by Clay Bridges Press in Houston, TX
www.ClayBridgesPress.com

All rights reserved. No part of this publication may be reproduced, stored in a retrieval system, or transmitted in any form by any means, electronic, mechanical, photocopy, recording, or otherwise, without the prior permission of the publisher, except as provided for by USA copyright law.

ISBN: 978-1-68488-115-4 Paperback
ISBN: 978-1-68488-116-1 Hardback
eISBN: 978-1-68488-117-8

Special Sales: Most Clay Bridges titles are available in special quantity discounts. Custom imprinting or excerpting can also be done to fit special needs. Contact Clay Bridges at Info@ClayBridgesPress.com

Auntie Says...
Quick Wisdom for Graduates
THE NEPHEW REVIEW

Contents

A Quick Heads-Up	v
Starting off Right but Ending up Wrong	v
Let's Start with Drinking . . .	1
Now, Let's Talk about Sex	17
Let's Talk about Sex: The Mother's Note (if I were your mother)	47
A Few Things Women Wish You Knew	49
Choices	61
Class and Academics	65
Own Your Time	79
The Resource of Money	91
Take Care of You	105
Security	111
Friends and Relationships	117
Social Media	139
Worship and Family	149
The Blessing	157
Acknowledgments	161
Citations	163

A Quick Heads-Up

Somebody probably gave you this book as a graduation gift. I bet you really wanted money, but don't be too hard on them. They want the best for you and thought what's in here could help you more than a few dollars.

Obviously, you don't have to read it if you don't want to. But you can read this whole book in the time it takes to watch one episode of your favorite Netflix series. If you'd like to make it even shorter, here are two suggestions:

1. Read through the titles, and go to the sections that interest you. If they're good, then read the rest.

2. Just read the "Auntie Says" statements. Don't get into the details unless something really grabs your attention.

As any auntie would, I pray the best for you and your transition into college and adulthood. If you have questions, give me a shout at auntie@myauntiesays.com, www.myauntiesays.com, or IG@myauntiesays.

God bless!

Starting off Right but Ending up Wrong

Graduating from high school and moving on to the next chapter of your life is a very big step. In our American culture, having that step land on a college campus is often what's expected and celebrated. Whether you know it or not, while your family members are celebrating, they're also breathing a collective sigh of relief. To them, you have shown you're planning ahead and making moves toward a life of career progression versus job changes. The concern that you won't "do something with your life" is off the table. In short, you just let them know that you've got it together.

But what if you don't?

I have a cousin named Byron. (His name is not Byron, but do you know how much trouble I'd get into if I used his real name?) Byron has been used to being the center of attention since he was little. He's an only child, has always been cute and smart, is naturally gifted at many things, and has a killer smile. His mom, aunts, uncles, teachers, church members—pretty much anybody who knows him—has always spoiled him.

When he began to show real promise on the football field, his head basically grew two sizes. I would label the way he carried himself as thinly veiled arrogance. But as far as he was concerned, he was the definition of an old Will Smith lyric—"I'm not conceited, I'm as good as I say I am."

About the time Byron was starting his junior year in high school, I saw him at a family reunion. Standing over the potato salad, I asked him a laid-back version of "what do you want to be when you grow up?" I admit I expected him to say something like going pro, getting an endorsement with Nike or Adidas, and moving from mansion to mansion as he shaped his dazzling football legacy. Along the way, I figured his ego would lead him through a string of wild spending sprees and sports groupies. Typical.

Instead, Byron's response gave me refreshing hope. He said he wanted to be an engineer. What? Since he was from Texas, he thought he might do something in oil and gas. He planned to play college football to fund his education. His mom couldn't afford to send him to college even with his dad kicking in what he could. If Byron made a pro team, that would be fine. But he'd still get a degree because knees and backs don't always let you be as great as you can be. "That can end a career quick," he said. Wow!

Byron was killin' it. His grades were great, and he'd already been scouted by four schools. Graduation came, and we celebrated. Byron went off to college, and we celebrated. Things were going really well.

Fast forward.

It was Sunday dinner at Aunt Kay's. Byron was sitting on the couch when I came in and set the mac 'n' cheese on the counter (yes, I am that aunt). I was immediately concerned because it was February, and he should be at school.

It turned out that Byron was home for the foreseeable future. Unfortunately, he had failed two classes, gotten a D in another, and was on academic probation. He lost his scholarship, had to move back home, and was now working at FedEx throwing boxes.

After some time at the domino table, Byron came out on the back porch and sat next to me. I asked how school was going (I didn't want him to know that someone had already told his business). He told me he was taking a break to rehab his shoulder and then left it at that.

Six months later, I got a little more detail. Byron had always been super smart, but in college he needed to put in real work and study to make good grades. He had figured that out, but he hadn't figured out how to study. On top of that, he wasn't always going to class and spent too much time drinking and hanging out. All that led to his transition from campus to FedEx. As cliché as it sounds, his dream of greatness had turned into a nightmare.

Okay, so he needed stronger study skills. But really, how did that happen? Well, I still haven't gotten Byron to answer that one, but if I had to guess:

- Byron got a couple low test grades, missed a few assignments, and didn't know what to do to get back on track.

- Instead of telling the whole truth to his mom, his dad, his coach, his advisor, or anybody, he acted like everything was okay and was determined to solve the problem on his own.

- He allowed his habit-turned-need to be the coolest one in the room to dictate:

- his relationships—characterized by sexual conquest (distracting and time-consuming).

- his class participation—characterized by low attendance (but he could often be found at the gym and the student union).

- his party attendance—(never missed one!).

- his drinking habits—characterized by an ever-growing collection of empty bottles (proudly displayed on the top shelf above his desk).

- He didn't have a real plan for how he would reach his goal to graduate from college.

- He let embarrassment stop him from getting help and getting back on his road to success.

Unfortunately for him, Byron had to leave his D1 school for a stop at a community college, followed by a full transfer to a state school. With no scholarship, he worked and piled up student loans.

The degree he finally earned did not come with the impressive network he would have benefited from at his first school, so he's in a mediocre gig waiting for something to give him a major career jump. And all that messin' around got him an anemic relationship with a girl he got pregnant, who promptly dropped out of college. The struggle is real.

I felt bad for Byron. I still do, even though he's pushing through and things are getting better. At the time, there wasn't really anything I could do for him.

But there is something I can do for you.

Let Auntie give you some knowledge that can help you avoid disasters like this and a few others.

Let's Start with Drinking . . .

Auntie Says

• • •

Alcohol can make you do some very stupid things.

Don't give up control of yourself.

• • •

I'm going to skip the statistics about alcohol-related deaths in 16-to-24-year-olds. I'm going to skip the lecture about not doing something just because your friends are doing it. I'm even going to hop over the talk about how expensive alcohol is. I'm going to skip all that and get straight to this:

> Alcohol can make you do some very stupid things. Don't give up control of yourself.

While buzzed, and definitely while drunk, you might:

- lose your wallet/keys/phone/(insert important item here) and have no earthly idea where to find them.

- not protect yourself when you have sex—which could get you a baby and/or a sexually transmitted infection.

- miss the signs and force yourself on someone— which could land you on the continuum between sexual assault and rape.

69% percent of sexual assault events involve alcohol use by the perpetrator.[1]

- become violent and physically assault someone.

- get jumped by some random dudes you don't even know.

American culture has told you two lies: (1) being wild and drunk is one of the only ways to really enjoy yourself, and (2) getting drunk is part of what you're supposed to do as a college student. Don't believe them.

Also, hangovers suck!

Auntie Says

• • •

Don't waste your
time, your money, or
your life getting high.

• • •

Just one joint seems harmless. It's "natural" and just "chills you out," so it's no big deal. Here's the part that no one tells you. Evidence has shown you will most likely:

- skip class and/or work.[2]
- have lower grades.[3]
- take longer to graduate.[4]

Do you know that marijuana can even lower your IQ—permanently?[5] In short, if you smoke weed, it is known to come with a range of negative side effects.[6] You will waste your time and your money, and you could waste your life.

So you'll only smoke on the weekends? That's also not a good idea. It can take up to 28 days for you to completely get back to your sharp self after you stop ingesting cannabis.[7] You restart that clock every time you smoke.

While we're on the subject, don't take pills, and don't do cocaine. The feeling—including the energy and focus you think you need to ace that test—will not be worth it. At the risk of sounding like a middle school video, let me say: it's a very slippery slope. You can quickly go from trying it, to using it only when you need it, to being completely strung out.

Save yourself the time and trouble of the downward spiral.

Studies show that frequent marijuana use and lower GPA are linked, even among students who thought their performance was not being affected.[8]

Auntie Says

• • •

Drinking to the point where you have no control of your own body is stupid.

• • •

Drinking to a point of diminished control makes you stupid because—

You. Could. Die.

Six people die of alcohol overdose each day.[9]

Don't be one of them.

It's easy to get caught up when you're partying, especially when you don't wanna look like a lightweight. But don't let your ego write a check that your body can't cash.

You generally start to reach the danger zone around four or five drinks within a two-hour period.[10] That's based on standard drinks (see the graphic below). You have to be even more careful with the punch at parties because you have no idea what's in it.

While I think it's best not to drink, you should be able to limit yourself to one or two standard drinks and still have a good time (make sure you eat a whole meal). Don't endanger your education, your relationships, your property, your character, or even your life by drinking so much that you're unsafe.

What Is a Standard Drink?[11]

12 fl oz of regular beer	8–10 fl oz of malt liquor or flavored malt beverages such as hard seltzer (shown in a 12 oz glass)	5 fl oz of table wine	3–4 fl oz of fortified wine (such as sherry or port; 3.5 oz shown)	2–3 fl oz of cordial, liqueur, or aperitif (2.5 oz shown)	1.5 fl oz of brandy or cognac (a single jigger or shot)	1.5 fl oz shot of distilled spirits (gin, rum, tequila, vodka, whiskey, etc.)
about 5% alcohol	about 7% alcohol	about 12% alcohol	about 17% alcohol	about 24% alcohol	about 40% alcohol	about 40% alcohol

Each drink shown above contains 0.6 fluid ounces of "pure" ethanol and represent one U.S. "standard drink" or "alcoholic drink equivalent."

What Does Alcohol Poisoning Look Like? [11]

- Mental confusion, stupor

- Difficulty remaining conscious, or inability to wake up

- Vomiting

- Seizures

- Slow breathing (fewer than 8 breaths per minute)

- Irregular breathing (10 seconds or more between breaths)

- Slow heart rate

- Clammy skin

- Dulled responses, such as no gag reflex (which prevents choking)

- Extremely low body temperature, bluish skin color or paleness

If someone is showing signs... call 911 immediately

Auntie Says

• • •

Don't think you can use being drunk or high as an excuse for your behavior.

You can't.

• • •

responsible for your actions.

...oxication as an explanation for what you did ...ten just an excuse.

...ople drink or smoke to take the edge off because they're nervous about doing or saying something. That choice can do two things: (1) give you a false sense of security and strength, and (2) leave you not in full control of yourself. The second result can produce very uncomfortable consequences. Intoxication lowers your inhibition, decreases your control, and affects your judgment.

Remember this:

> When you give control of yourself to a substance, you pay the consequences for what you did while it was in control.

Don't let that be you.

Auntie Says

• • •

I promise: You can still be the strong man you want to be if you choose not to drink or get high.

• • •

Because you are a man, you can *choose* not to drink alcohol. You can *choose* not to get high. You may decide to stand on the fact that you want to stay in control, that you don't like the taste, that it doesn't work with your body chemistry, or that it's against your religion. But no explanation is needed. Maybe you just "don't drink or smoke."

You should be able to decide and stand on what you choose for you. What if your friends keep pushing you to indulge? What if they give you a hard time because you won't explain to their satisfaction why you won't drink or smoke? Well, you may need new friends.

Auntie Says

• • •

If you're always
drinking or smoking,
you may need help.

• • •

you find that you're always drunk, drinking, high, ...ing, or taking pills every day, you are likely self-medicating. You may need help to get healthy and feel better. You may not need AA or NA yet, but spending some time talking to a counselor is likely a very good choice for you. Please do so before someone gets hurt.

Your college tuition pays for both mental and physical health services. Use them.

If you need help, you can use services on campus or visit https://www.samhsa.gov/find-treatment. Or call 800.662.4357 for help with alcohol or drug problems, or for mental health support.

Now, Let's Talk about Sex

Auntie Says

• • •

Sex changes you, and you can't always anticipate how.

• • •

Each time you have sex, you are changed mentally and spiritually. No matter what you keep telling yourself, you cannot control or predict every outcome.

You might get more attached than you intend to or expect.

- Will you actually miss her when she's not around, even if you're not in a relationship?
- Will you look completely desperate as you troll social media?

You could stop valuing the spiritual connection of physical intimacy.

- What if this is the start of losing your ability to fully connect with your future wife?

Your thoughts of previous encounters could come back when you definitely don't want them to.

- What happens when she starts popping up in your dreams while you're involved with someone else?
- What do you do when those thoughts come back—when you're with your wife 10 years later—and say the wrong name?

You may pick up something.

- Genital warts? Herpes? Chlamydia?

Or you may leave something behind.

- What if one industrious sperm starts you on a baby journey before you even know about it?

Sperm can remain alive in the female reproductive tract for up to five days past ejaculation.[12]

There are a lot of things that could go the wrong way. Are you comfortable with that?

Auntie Says

• • •

Don't be in a hurry if
you haven't done it.

• • •

Don't be in a rush to have sex if you haven't, even if you believe everyone else on the planet has. It's okay. There's a lot more to life and relationships than sex.

But you may not want to tell the whole world that you're a virgin. Our society expects that you'll be very sexually active, and you likely know many people who are. So it makes sense if you want to keep that to yourself.

If you've chosen not to have sex or even to stop having sex while you focus on your education, stick to your convictions. Do not let pop culture or your friends tell you what kind of man you should be. That's between you and God.

Auntie Says

• • •

Porn is not good for you.

• • •

No matter what your eyes and your friends tell you, porn is unhealthy for you.

Porn sets unrealistic expectations for how relationships work, how sex works, what you should look like naked, what she should look like naked, and how adults behave.

Yes, it probably excites you because it is sexual, and as a guy, you're most likely very visual. However, it's kind of like eating moldy cake. It's very sweet—too sweet—and the texture is kind of off. But since you're eating cake, you think it's all good. Then later, your stomach is a mess, and you're hurling. After that, you're still hungry.

In a 2014 study, 53.5 percent of porn-consuming males ages 16 to 21 exhibited one or more of the following sexual dysfunctions:[13]

- Erectile dysfunction
- Difficulty orgasming
- Low sexual desire

These problems, historically associated with men over 40 or men with other psychological or physical factors, have the potential to be reversible by quitting pornography.

You may be thinking: "I don't want to watch porn to be aroused; I want to watch it to learn about sex." If you need to learn more, watch credible documentaries, or read a few instructional books. Watching is not worth risking your sexual, psychological, or relationship health.

If you can't stop watching porn, if you're losing large chunks of time watching it, or if you're hiding the fact that you watch it, call 800.662.4357 or text 435748.

Auntie Says

• • •

Consent is real
and *required*.

• • •

Okay, let's get this straight once and for all.

You may believe her body is saying "yes," but if her mouth says "no"—even once, even a whisper, even if her eyes are closed and she looks happy, even if she already said "yes"—**You Stop.**

>   After a "no," if you press forward with physical activity, you are committing sexual assault.

>   After a "no," if you press forward with sexual activity, you are committing rape.

Getting consent is simple and necessary.

One way is to ask, "Is this okay?" When you're moving from holding her hand to kissing her, when you're moving from kissing her to touching her, and most definitely when you're moving from any of this to sexual activity, you pause at each of these points and ask, "Is this okay?"

If her answer is ever "no," you back up without anger to the last thing that was okay. If that means your physical touch time is over, then it's over. Do not become a sex offender because you don't use the strength to control yourself.

Auntie Says

• • •

Consent can be withdrawn. Her "yes" can become a "no," and *you have to respect it.*

• • •

Let me be clear. If she has said "yes" the entire time and you're finally at the point of penetration, and then she says "no"—**You Stop.**

If you are two minutes into sexual intercourse and she says "no" or "stop"—**You Stop.**

It will be difficult. You will not be happy. But this is how it's supposed to work.

If it makes you feel any better, it goes the other way too. She should respect your body and your right to decide what happens to it, just like you respect hers.

Two more things:

1. If you're unsure that everything is a "go" or she looks at all uncomfortable, ask if what you're doing is okay. If she says "no" or gives an unsure response—**You Stop.** You don't want to misinterpret the signs, hurt someone, and possibly end up with disciplinary action against you.

2. Do not ever pressure someone to have sex with you. Do not offer to trade something (a handbag, concert tickets, a nice dinner, etc.) for sex. Ask nicely if it's okay. If she says "no," **You Stop.**

Auntie Says

• • •

Don't pimp someone's daughter.

• • •

If you wouldn't pimp your mother or your sister, don't pimp someone else's.

If you're running a side hustle hooking people up and getting anything of value because of it, you're pimping someone's daughter. Stop it.

Auntie Says

• • •

Absolutely no sex without latex.

• • •

DO NOT have sex without a condom!

Side note: If I were your auntie in real life, I would tell you not to do it at all. It's distracting and outside your God-honoring values, and it exposes you to some very unpleasant consequences. That said, if you choose to have sex, this info (and more in this section) is for you.

It doesn't matter who she is, how much y'all "love" each other, how long y'all have been together, how much you don't like condoms, how much she doesn't like condoms, whether she's on birth control, or if you're sure you can get her to take a Plan B.

If you don't commit to wearing a condom and stick to it—without fail—you are elevating your desires (or hers) above what's best for you. The rest of your life going the way you planned is on the line.

If she doesn't want a condom because she's determined to get the "real" you, pack it up and take a hard pass. She may have another agenda that you do not want any part of.

If either of you is allergic to latex, there are several other types of condoms available at the health service on your campus. Or you can get them at Target, Walmart, grocery stores, and even gas stations. If they're all closed, it's a sign—go home alone.

Auntie Says

• • •

Have fresh condoms,
and take care of them.

• • •

Do *not* rely on that old box of condoms you bought in your junior year of high school.

The age and type of condoms, and the spermicide that may be in them, can contribute to their degradation. To be safe, *do not use a condom that is more than two years old.*

Protect your protection. Because high or prolonged heat and temperature swings are bad for condoms:

- Do not leave them in cars.

- If you accidentally run them through the washer and dryer, throw them away immediately.

- Avoid keeping them in your wallet or up against your phone because heat gets trapped there.

Maintain your own protection. Do not rely on your friend to keep the condom stash. You don't know where he got them or if he's been protecting his protection.

Never leave home with just one condom. Things happen, and you may need a backup. You don't want to get in a situation where you feel you have to have sex without one.

Learn the right way to put on a condom. Before you need to wear one, search plannedparenthood.org or google "how to put on a condom" to be sure you'll do it correctly.

It may sound like Auntie's overreacting, but you take your future in your hands (well, not really your hands) every time you have sex. You could damage your health and/or create a life. Either of these could drastically change the course you have planned for your own life.

Don't take it lightly.

Auntie Says

• • •

Listen for the
pop. Condoms break.

• • •

Pay attention! Be sure you don't hear the condom pop. That does happen, and it immediately puts you at serious risk for sexually transmitted infections (STIs) and pregnancy.

If you hear it, stop immediately, and get another one. Do not get drawn into how good it feels or wave it off because "we might as well go on without it now since it already broke." You are asking for trouble. Even if she wants to keep going, stop and get another condom. (See why I told you never to go with just one condom?)

It may be a little awkward, but before you have sex, the two of you should get on the same page about what y'all will do if this happens so no mid-sex conversation is necessary.

By the way, this is another time when alcohol or drugs can affect your judgment and cost you. At least one in five college students abandons safe sex practices when they're drunk, even if they protect themselves when they're sober.[14]

One study of college students found that 29% of male condom appliers had experienced at least one broken condom over the past three months.[15]

Auntie Says

• • •

Don't let the
sex blind you.

• • •

Many a man has been blinded by sex. Sometimes it's like you can't think straight—and I'm not even talking about when her clothes are off.

It can significantly impact your non-sexual interactions. You may overlook and accept things like these:

- Toxic attitudes and behavior
- Basic expectations not being met
- Destructive habits
- Not being sure she's exclusive with you even though y'all are supposed to be

Men are not the only ones who sometimes enter relationships only for their own benefit. You could end up being one of several guys paying for her lifestyle and keeping her happy sexually. Is that what you want?

Choose sexual activity based on your values. Be careful how much power and access you give someone with no binding commitment to you.

Auntie Says

• • •

If you get her pregnant,
I promise you the
sex will *not*
have been worth it.

• • •

I know you may be used to this kind of statement being directed at females, but it applies to you too.

Having a baby is not easy. Taking care of a baby is even harder. Raising an entire human being is even harder than that. If you choose not to walk away from the responsibility of an unplanned pregnancy and to put in the work to take care of and raise the child, you will be amazed at how hard it is.

If you're right there with her and the baby, you will sacrifice the luxuries you can buy and the ones you cannot (like sleeping as late as you want, spending all your money on whatever you want, not having to worry about feeding anyone but yourself). You will likely feel frustrated, confused, afraid, tired, and ready to take the pressure off by moving on.

A pregnancy is not something you can just erase with no consequences. The sex will *not* have been worth it.

Auntie Says

• • •

If you get her pregnant, be the responsible man you know you should be.

• • •

You may not even want to entertain discussion of having a baby. You're young, and you have your whole life ahead of you. Well, those facts should have convinced you not to expose yourself to the risk of pregnancy. It's too late now. Be a man, and be responsible. Sit down with her and possibly her parents, your parents, a counselor, a pastor, or another responsible adult, and have the grown-up conversations to decide what you're going to do.

If y'all decide to have the baby, there are a few options. You can choose to raise the baby together or separately. You can choose to put the baby up for adoption. If you choose adoption, it's possible to choose the parents and have open or closed relationships with them and/or the child. Whatever you choose, commit to walk it out even when it's difficult.

If y'all decide to have an abortion,* be there! It's easier and a real option for you not to show up—but don't be that guy. Because you were present when the life was created, you should be present for this too. Contribute financially, be present at the facility during the procedure, and, if she'll allow you to, be there for support while she's recovering. She has taken on all the risk and pain, and she will likely carry the mental burden in a way you never can. This is your part—do it.

A word of caution: Don't be in such a hurry to take a Plan B or have an abortion. They're not always as successful or easy as some people say they are (for either of you). Take the time to investigate all your options.

If she's pregnant and you need help and answers, try www.nrlc.org 800.712.4357, www.optionline.org 866.993.0794, or text 313131 to chat with someone.

---

*Auntie strongly suggests you choose any option but this one. Life is sacred, and there are many people willing and able to take care of the baby if you cannot.

Auntie Says

• • •

Hooking up can get
you hooked before
you realize it...
and not in a good way.

• • •

If you engage in casual sex and do so regularly, you can probably expect her to be in her feelings about you and to let you know it. Hooking up may not be as easy or enjoyable as it sounds once real emotion and relationship expectations are in play.

What else may surprise you? It's the two ways your feelings about your partners are likely to go. You can either be the stereotypical guy who is emotionless and free or the atypical guy who has strong emotions entangled in these connections.

Emotionless Guy runs the risk of gradually losing the ability to have healthy romantic connections. This sounds like a good thing to a guy who wants to use women as interchangeable entertainment and sexual gratification. But if Emotionless Guy ever wants to have a stable long-term relationship, a strong marriage, or a healthy parenting partnership, he may be securing his failure with all his empty sexual successes.

Passionate Guy risks being weighed down by his unexpected emotional connections. The humanity that drives his feelings is admirable. He doesn't think women are just the sum of their parts or that they only exist for his amusement and pleasure. But Passionate Guy can wear himself out with too much feeling focus, resulting in not being prepared to develop relationships with intention that grow into strong connections over time.

Sexual intercourse—like anything else that can alter who you are and the course your life—should be chosen carefully and according to your values. Choose wisely.

Auntie Says

• • •

Try talking without sex. It's cleaner and less complicated.

• • •

Just because you're talking to someone doesn't mean you have to have sex with them—especially before you define the relationship.

If you think you do, in a way that's not your fault. Every series and movie you watch makes it seem normal to:

   A. Pull up on someone and *maybe* learn their first name.

   B. Have a drink.

   C. Have sex.

The lack of seriousness and sex without commitment are attractive. But that's not how it's supposed to be.

It should be more like this:

   A. Pull up on someone and *definitely* learn their first name.

   B. Have a drink or eat something, or just kick it.

   C. Do some non-sexual things to see if you enjoy being with this person.

   D. Start to learn who she is, what she likes and doesn't, what she believes and doesn't, how she treats people, how she is with money and without it, what her temper is like, and more.

You can't decide if this relationship is worth your time and focus if you jump right into sex.

Try studying together at the library. Have lunch, get coffee, or watch a movie. Do you see how sex was not on that list? Do these kinds of things until you start to build an actual relationship.

And another thing—if you just keep grabbing new girls to scratch your sexual itch, you may learn two things:

1. The itch you're trying to scratch physically is actually a heart-thing that sex will *never* satisfy.

2. You may end up with an itch (like an STI) that you can never get rid of.

Let's Talk about Sex:
The Mother's Note
(if I were your mother)

Dear, *(insert your name here)*,

I love you **dearly**, and I have **absolutely zero intention** to raise your child. Also, I **will not** hold onto him or her until you finish school or be your built-in-Monday-through-Friday babysitter.

Do not take my unwillingness to take over your parenting responsibility as an excuse to walk away from it or the little life you created.

Even if the baby's mother agrees to keep the baby most of the time and therefore agrees to do most of the work, your life will be irreparably changed and harder. You will definitely feel the weight of the consequences of your choices and the sacrifices it will take to fulfill them before the baby is out of diapers. It will be harder still if you have the child full-time. In any case, you will need to put money, time, effort, and love into raising your child.

I will love you the entire time. I will love my grandchild and will work to not make him or her pay for your actions. I will provide an appropriate level of grandmotherly assistance, but I will not enable you.

Love,

Mama

A Few Things Women Wish You Knew

Auntie Says

• • •

Please just take a shower.

• • •

Stop believing you can use body spray or cologne to cover up the past day (or days). It doesn't matter if you're in a hurry or you think to yourself, "I haven't done anything today." Take a shower!

You need to take a full shower at least once every 24 hours.

And yes, it's ridiculous for me to say this, but I'm saying it anyway—three things:

1. Use soap.

2. Wash everything.

3. Scrub.

While you're at it, clean your fingernails. You don't have to get a manicure; just clean them. Did you know that if you scratch them on a soapy washcloth in that shower we just talked about, you'll clean them effortlessly and quickly? Weird, but true.

Auntie Says

• • •

Clean your room.

• • •

No woman who respects herself wants to hang out in the smelly, messy, potentially pest-infested pigpen you're calling your room—and you shouldn't either.

Have more respect for yourself.

Besides, you have to admit that it takes a long time to find anything in there. You've probably lost a shoe, at least one shirt, and a charging cord just today.

And yes, if you're off campus, this applies to your entire apartment, especially the kitchen and the bathroom.

Auntie Says

• • •

Gaming is not life. Football is not life. (Your favorite thing) is not life.

Broaden your horizons.

• • •

Bring something to the table. No woman wants a man who can only speak intelligently about what he likes and does. That means you need to know about more than just what you do, eat, watch, and play.

Seek to understand concepts in class instead of just memorizing what you need to pass a test.

Build on your interest in useful, non-academic areas.

Engage in enriching, pleasurable activities. Read a decent book every once in a while. Then read another decent book that is a different genre than the last one. Listen to a well-produced podcast—or three.

Put more into yourself than empty pleasure interests (e.g., hours of scrolling through Instagram or TikTok, extended gaming sessions, etc.). Then you'll have something more to pour out when you finally spend time with her.

Auntie Says

• • •

She's probably gonna eat some of your food, and she doesn't want you to be mad about it.

• • •

No one knows why, but sometimes even after a woman has declared herself "not hungry," the smell and look of your food changes her mind just a little bit. When this happens, she hopes you want to please her enough and care for her enough to happily share with her. You show that by not getting mad, by being generous, and by giving her a little something to eat. You should also share your feelings about it, but be kind when you do.

If you are the kind of guy who gets really bothered when you don't get to eat all your food, add a little something to the order so you'll be covered. For a while, there was a restaurant not far from my house whose last menu item was named, "My Girlfriend's Not Hungry." It consisted of two chicken wings and a few fries. I bet that solved this problem for many a boyfriend.

Auntie Says

• • •

She'll respect and
trust you more if
you always tell the truth.

• • •

Have you noticed it's very difficult to give genuine respect to someone who is lying or cheating every time you turn around (even if they're not doing it to you)? Not surprisingly, it's also hard to be vulnerable with or depend on that person.

Women want to know they can trust you to be who you really are, even with your faults and mistakes. Your best self wants to be someone who earns respect and can be trusted—a man who is honest, speaks his mind, treats others with respect, works hard to earn what he gets, keeps his commitments, and so on.

Be honest with yourself and others. For example:

- If you're not interested in being exclusive, tell her right up front.

- If you want to end a relationship, communicate clearly and compassionately.

- If you make a mistake, own it with honest conversation.

- If you need an "A," get tutored and study; don't steal the test.

- If you're on a group project, do your share of the work with excellence.

- Only commit to others what you are willing and able to do.

- Tell the truth even when it hurts, but do it kindly.

I think you get the point. If you're this guy, you can leave your phone on the table when you go to the bathroom, and she won't even look at it—okay, maybe once ☺.

Choices

Auntie Says

• • •

Consistently choose to be true to the best version of yourself.

• • •

While in college, you will likely be in another city and responsible for yourself. Your parents and family will not know every choice you make, but God will.

Make choices that will make God and you proud.

Make choices that reflect the best parts of your upbringing, your value system, and your spiritual education.

If you do that, I promise you will have a happier, richer, more productive life. You won't miss out on as much as you think you will. What you do miss will not be nearly as great as you think it will be.

Classes and Academics

Auntie Says

• • •

Unless you're dying or contagious, go to class!

• • •

Go to class! Unless you are sick and cannot function or are contagious, go to class!

Before you go to class, it really helps to read the material that will be covered, watch the previous session, and reread (not skim) notes from the last class. Why?

- Reviewing material, especially on the same day it was or will be covered in class, helps reinforce the information.

- If you've already introduced yourself to what the prof will cover, you can ask questions during class and listen to understand. You won't let information go in one ear and out the other or scramble to keep up with taking notes. Either way, you miss something. This is likely one reason you're clueless during the test.

- Knowing what's going on helps keep you awake.

- Being lost in class can make you say to yourself, "I'm not learning anything anyway." At that point, you block it all out and have no chance of learning anything at all—another reason you're clueless during the test.

Auntie Says

• • •

When you get that *first* low homework, quiz, or test grade, get help immediately.

• • •

Don't ignore the signs that you're in academic trouble. Remember, grades are indicators of two things: (1) how well you're doing what's required for the class and (2) how well you've mastered the material.

When your grades drop below your true potential (most people do actually have the potential to get A's), take steps to correct whatever is out of whack. Those steps could include the following:

- Make sure you check off each requirement for every assignment.

- Raise the neatness or detail level of your work.

- Visit your professor during office hours and get your questions answered (bonus: your professor will know you're putting in effort and may give you a little more grace).

- Do more practice problems.

- Get tutoring more than once a week.

- Make flash cards by hand (muscle memory actually does help).

- Review your notes before bed the same night you take them.

- Do whatever you know works to get you back on track.

Auntie Says

• • •

Every semester: Know the class drop deadline, and respect its power.

• • •

Always be aware of the last date you can drop a class. Put it on your calendar, and evaluate your chances of doing well in the class at least two weeks before that date.

Dropping a class is a pretty serious thing. You can't drop every class that is difficult or inconvenient. If you do that, you'll never finish school.

If you have study partners and tutoring help available, don't jump ship if you don't have to. You may not have those supports if you take the class later. But, if you have to drop because you are honestly overloaded with too many intense classes, you'll have to catch it later and pray up some help.

Also, you should not underestimate and should always investigate the potential negative impacts of dropping even one class. Sometimes classes are only offered in certain semesters. That means you may have to go to summer school (more $) or wait an entire year to take the class again. If you drop a class that's a prerequisite for something else you need, your whole situation is on hold until you pass that class. Check with your advisor to make sure you don't miss out on these details.

If necessary, it is definitely worth shutting down a section of your social life for a semester so you can sharpen your focus and pass a class. It'll suck for a little while, but it's a more mature choice than running from the challenge. And that class will be off your plate.

Auntie Says

• • •

Use your academic advisor. You're already paying for them, and they can be very valuable to you.

• • •

Meet with your advisor, and take it seriously. Prepare for the meeting.

What should you talk about? I'm so glad you asked. Ask them to do these things:

- Walk you through your degree plan and advise you on any changes or choices you need to make.

- Find career resources that give specific examples on how or where you can use your degree and how much money you'll make doing each.

- Help you find professionals in a few of those jobs that you can shadow.

- Help you find internships and summer job connections during your first or second meeting in the fall (don't wait until the last minute when everyone else does it).

- Recommend professors who can help find or provide internships, summer jobs, research opportunities, or work for you during the school year.

Do not be afraid to ask them to do some leg work to make sure you're aiming your efforts in the right direction. It's their job. If they say it's not, ask whose job it is and make an appointment to see that person.

Get your questions answered so every year you can make the most of the opportunities you have while you're in college.

By the way, this approach can also work with a manager or human resources representative at work. Feel free to ask them how you can prepare for growth in your current job, get a potential promotion, or change your career path. All these can benefit you and the company.

Auntie Says

• • •

Don't study where
you sleep.

• • •

If you can help it, don't study in your dorm room or bedroom if you're in an apartment.

You might think that leaving your room opens you up to being derailed, but here's the secret no one tells you:

80 percent of the distractions are in your own space.

If you leave, you only have to fight off the other 20 percent.

Auntie Says

• • •

If your phone is not
silenced and out
of sight, you're not
really studying.

• • •

Your mom was right about this one. If you don't need your phone to actually do the studying, you'll be more productive if you can't hear or see it at all while you're trying to study.

Set screen time or app limits through your settings, or silence everything except the alarm you're using as a timer. Then put your phone inside a drawer or backpack, or anywhere except in front of you. Turning it face down is not enough.

It's exceedingly difficult to maintain complete focus while subconsciously keeping an eye or ear out for the next notification. When you receive it, your study train of thought is derailed and has to be reestablished every time. I know, you think that's only an issue for old people, but it's not.

Just try it for a week and see.

And no, you don't have to tell me I was right. I already know.

> Studies show just having our phones nearby makes us perform worse, but we don't realize it's having an effect. The recommendation? Silence it or turn it off, and put it in another room to improve your focus.[16]

Own Your Time

Auntie Says

• • •

Spend time like money. Use a schedule to stay on track.

• • •

Creating and following a schedule during the week will feel like too much work. And the weekends were made to have no schedule, right? Um—no.

When you have a lot of time and no structure, usually you get a lot of nothing done. That's not good for you. You have a lot on your plate. You have to find time to work hard, play hard, and rest hard.

The key is planning before the day arrives. You can plan for each day in the morning or in the night before. Planning for the week on Sunday or Monday works well too.

I suggest you start with block scheduling (see the example in this section). It will give you some basic structure so you don't suddenly realize that your time is all gone. It's not a good feeling.

Remember to include things related to these:

- Academics – class, studying, breaks, study groups, professor office hours, tutoring, meetings with your advisor

- Hygiene – you gotta take a shower and brush your teeth

- Self-care – workouts, walks, naps, reading, podcasts

- Chores – laundry, cleaning

- Nourishment – cooking, grocery shopping, cafeteria meals

- Spiritual/mental health – worship, counseling sessions, meditation, study

- Clothing maintenance – clothes and shoes shopping

- Social life – meetings and activities for organizations you join, friends, parties, romantic relationships

- Etc.

See? You don't have time for the hangover recovery I talked about in the "Let's Start with Drinking" section.

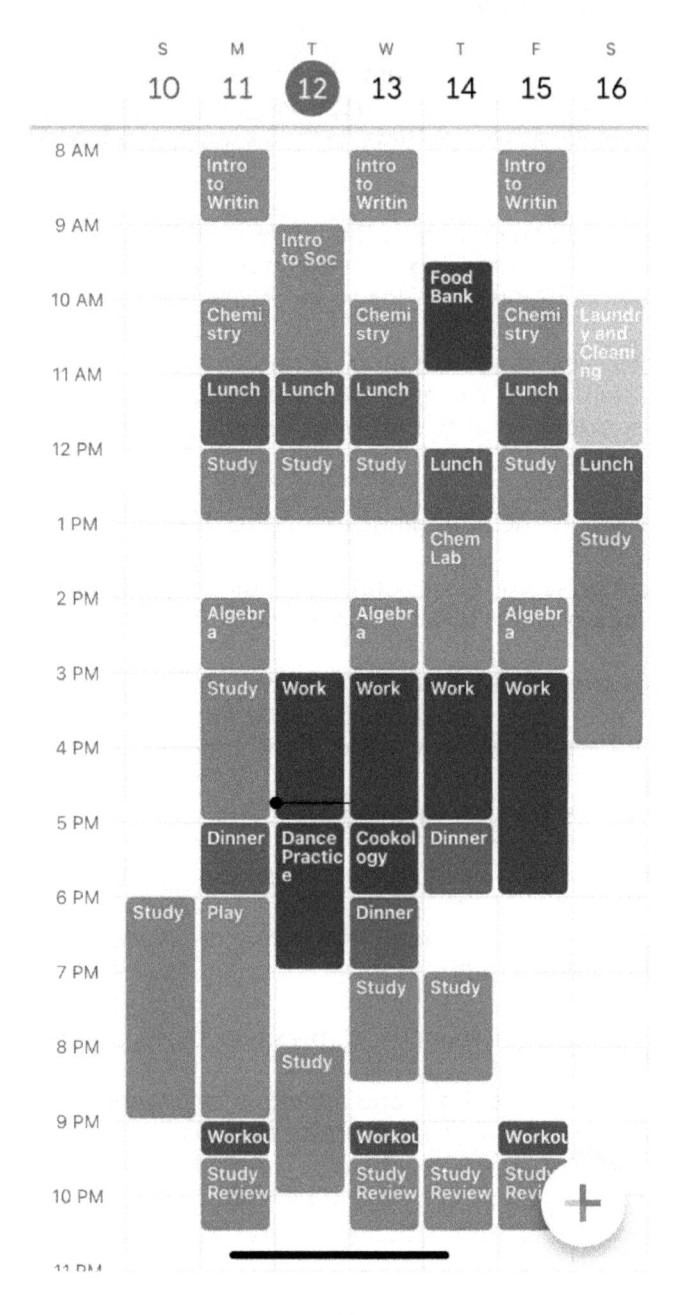

	S 10	M 11	T 12	W 13	T 14	F 15	S 16
8 AM		Intro to Writin		Intro to Writin		Intro to Writin	
9 AM			Intro to Soc				
10 AM		Chemistry		Chemistry	Food Bank	Chemistry	Laundry and Cleaning
11 AM		Lunch	Lunch	Lunch		Lunch	
12 PM		Study	Study	Study	Lunch	Study	Lunch
1 PM					Chem Lab		Study
2 PM		Algebra		Algebra		Algebra	
3 PM		Study	Work	Work	Work	Work	
4 PM							
5 PM		Dinner	Dance Practice	Cookology	Dinner		
6 PM	Study	Play		Dinner			
7 PM				Study	Study		
8 PM			Study				
9 PM		Workout		Workout		Workout	
10 PM		Study Review		Study Review	Study Review	Study Review	
11 PM							

Auntie Says

• • •

Set goals.

• • •

Develop goals, and do something to achieve them **every** day (at least every weekday).

At a minimum, have three short-term (zero to six months), three mid-term (six months to a year), and three long-term (up to three years) goals. By the time you graduate, you should be able to add at least one five-year goal.

By setting goals, you're creating an environment that's always looking forward with expectation, not dread. You want to have something to work toward and an achievement to celebrate.

Since your goals should reflect and inspire you, not all of them should come from external sources (e.g., your class syllabus, work requirements, parent demands, internship programs). It's your life, and you should proactively choose where you're headed. Circumstances and new information will come that will sometimes drive you to edit a goal or two, and that's okay. Adjust, and keep going.

In addition to basic goals like getting at least six hours of sleep a night and making a new schedule every semester, here are a few examples of what I'm talking about.

Target Completion	Goal
0 - 6 mos	• Learn how to get an internship at Frito Lay • Save for iPad
6 mos - 1 yr	• Maintain 3.5 GPA or higher • Buy iPad and use for all class notes
1 yr - 3 yr	• Start internship at Frito Lay • Pledge a service-based fraternity

Here's one more thing—your goals should be achievable but not a cakewalk. If it's too easy, will it even be worth celebrating when you achieve it?

Auntie Says

• • •

Don't let your goals
become daydreams.

• • •

"No man can win every battle, but no man should fall without a struggle" (Peter Parker in *Spider-Man: Homecoming*). Translation: put in some work! Don't let your circumstances and your limitations overwhelm you without thinking, working, and finding resources to overcome them. That's how you keep your goals from dwindling to daydreams.

Here's **how to be more successful** at reaching your goals:

1. **Write down your goals.** Use a plain piece of notebook paper and post your goals on the wall, or create a note on your phone, or use a spiral notebook just for goals. Writing them down increases the chance you'll achieve them.

2. Whether it's daily, weekly, or a couple times a month, **consistently take real steps toward each of your goals.** Break them down, put the steps in spots on your schedule or to-do lists, and stay at it.

3. **Review your goals regularly.** When you start this habit, review your goals frequently. (I knew a guy who looked at his goals list several times a day during his entire freshman year). Once they're established, you may settle into weekly or monthly reviews.

Reviewing your goals regularly (#3) is an easy one to let slide. Don't. At an absolute minimum, you should review your goals once per semester. Here's a thought: review them the day before every finals week. If you tie the review to a regular date, a day of the week, or an event, you're less likely to forget.

By the way, the review is not meant to make you feel bad if you haven't reached a goal. It's meant to keep you on track so your pursuit of your goals will be a regular part of your decision-making process. How can you expect to make choices and take actions that help you accomplish your goals if you don't keep them on your mind?

Auntie Says

· · ·

Take pics of tutoring times and office hours.

· · ·

Snap pics or screenshots of your class tutoring times and professor office hours. Then save them in one album on your phone.

If you're having trouble in a class, have questions, or just want your professors to see you as more committed, you'll need to go to them. You may be more likely to show up and take advantage of these opportunities when you don't have to hunt for the information.

You should also consider taking pics of the full syllabus for each class (even though they're online). If you need to check something out, you'll be more likely to do it if you don't have to spend time searching.

The Resource of Money

Auntie Says

• • •

Credit cards are the devil!

Well, not really, but avoid them for now.

• • •

Say **no** to **all** credit cards, at least until your sophomore year. Whatever freebie you get will not be worth the debt you will probably accumulate, the bad habits you will probably develop, and the damage you will likely do to your credit. *All those things can follow you for years to come and keep you from living your best life.*

Do not believe them when they say you need to start developing a credit history by getting your first credit card now. They only care about signing up new accounts.

There is some truth to the position that later it is advantageous to have a credit history. But it needs to be a good credit history.

You may not yet have the skills, resources, or self-control to build and maintain responsible spending habits. When you don't, you generally become a person with bad credit. People with bad credit pay more for almost everything (e.g., higher interest rates on loans, credit cards, and car purchases, and larger deposits for utilities and apartments). They also have a harder time getting things they need (e.g., apartment leases, some jobs, auto loans, etc.).

No one wants bad credit, but to avoid it, you have to be intentional about how you acquire and use credit.

It may take some time to build healthy practices around spending and planning to use money. That doesn't often happen during your first year out of high school. You're focused on adjusting to the freedom, the responsibility, the social scene, the academic work, the time management requirements, and blah, blah, blah of your new life.

Use this year to train yourself to use your money wisely, and then we can talk about credit cards.

Auntie Says

• • •

Make your money behave. Use a spending plan.

• • •

Use a spending plan, and track your spending. At first it will suck if you feel restricted by the limits, but it will get easier and save you in the long run. If you don't limit and track your spending, you will overspend.

There are dozens of simple, free, or paid apps that will help with this, including Mint, PocketGuard, NerdWallet, and YNAB (You Need a Budget). Pick one, and get it going. If you don't like it, pick another one.

Just get started building this good habit. You'll be glad you did.

A year from now, you will wish you had started today.

Auntie Says

• • •

Don't leave money
on the table.

• • •

You will likely never again have the intersection of so much available money and so few requirements on its use. Take advantage of that.

Two things:

1. Apply for scholarships like it's your job!

2. Do not believe the unspoken lie that scholarship application time is over when you graduate from high school. There are plenty of scholarships you can earn directly from your school and outside sources even after your freshman year begins and beyond.

Any money left over after paying tuition and fees can be used for books and other expenses. You want that pile of money to be as big as possible, so get on it!

An estimated $100 million in scholarship money is left unawarded each year. Chief reason: lack of applicants.[17]

Auntie Says

• • •

Loan refunds are not free money. Use them wisely and save some, because college isn't forever.

• • •

If you get a loan refund (*bless you!*), take 10–50 percent of it, and put it into a savings vehicle (preferably one that is interest-bearing). Or better yet, invest it in an index fund that follows the S&P 500. Then **forget it exists until at least five years after you graduate**.

If you do this every year, you may have enough to pay off any school loans in 10 years or fewer after graduation.

You can also use this chunk of money to help with a down payment on your first home, your first investment property, the start of your first business, and more.

Don't go for short-term satisfaction on this one. Money is supposed to be a little tight in college; it's part of the experience. Do yourself a favor. Play the long game, and make those extra dollars do some work for you after you graduate.

You can make a dollar out of fifteen cents if you save and invest.

Auntie Says

• • •

Don't spend it all!

• • •

Spend less than you make, have, or receive. When you spend every last dime, that's called "living at the end of your means." Here's the worst part about that. When something that doesn't always happen happens, you have to rely on borrowing to keep up. If you don't have extra money to handle the unexpected thing, how will you have the money to pay back what you borrowed (or charged on the credit card I told you not to get)? How will you stay current with your regular expenses? And what's gonna happen when the next unexpected thing happens? That's one way to guarantee you'll build a truckload of debt that follows you for years.

After many financial bumps and bruises, several of which occurred during my college years, I learned 10/10/80—10 percent to the Lord/the church or to help others; 10 percent to save; and 80 percent to live on.

Now that I'm more exposed, educated, and experienced, I know that if you could live on 10 percent and give, save, and invest the rest, that would be awesome! That's not usually possible, so try one of the models in the table below. The larger you can make the save and invest buckets, the more financially prepared and comfortable you'll be in your future.

Financial Models to Prepare for Your Future	Lord/ Help Others	Save	Invest	Living Expenses*
Aggressive	15%	20%	25%	40%
Moderate	10%	15%	20%	55%
Conservative	10%	10%	5%	75%

*Living expenses are things such as tuition, books, rent, utilities, groceries, fuel, transportation, cell service, clothing, and fun money. Fun money includes nails, hair, streaming services, and anything else you want but don't actually need to live and further your college education or work life.

If you consistently save and invest, you will be amazed at how much money you'll have five or 10 years after graduation, mostly due to the discipline to leave the money alone.

Auntie Says

• • •

Don't spend your money

on stupid stuff.

• • •

Stop buying so much stuff! You don't need the newest version of everything all the time. Every year you're on campus, you have to pack it, move it, pay to store it—you're just throwing your coins away.

Check yourself. Are you always buying new clothes and shoes, new games, ordering food, Ubering everywhere, paying for dates and gifts, feeding your friends, and more? In a year, you won't want to wear half the stuff you bought, and you won't remember two-thirds of the stuff you did. Then what? You have nothing to move forward with in exchange for all the money you spent.

I know you want to look good, eat good, and have a good time. Those things are great, and sometimes you'll need money to do them. But you have to exercise some self-control.

Start by making your spending plan. The YNAB app is great for this. It can walk you through what a budget is, how to stick to it, and how to find ways to save and invest that you might not see.

Then work to think differently about what to spend your money on. Do you really need another pair of shoes, or should you save that money to invest, buy your next textbook, or pay for the cruise you want to take next summer?

Whatever you choose to spend it on, remember that there's only so much money to go around. You have to prioritize. You're not a little kid anymore, so more and more of your money will need to be spent on responsibilities, not just fun stuff.

Take Care of You

Auntie Says

• • •

Guys need self-care too.

• • •

Your health is on a short list of things that cannot be purchased or replaced, and it directly impacts everything else. Take care of you.

Don't hesitate to take advantage of health care—for both your physical and mental health.

If you have something on your body that doesn't look or feel right, go see a doctor at the student health service (which your tuition pays for). While you're waiting, make a note of your symptoms and when you started having them. They're gonna ask you for that info.

Do not downplay or ignore your mental health because you feel weird about it. If you broke your finger playing basketball, you wouldn't be ashamed to go to the doctor for help; you'd make it a priority and get it done. Respond the same way about your mental health. If you're feeling overwhelmed, angry, or lonely all the time; if you can't stop drinking; if you can't stay focused while you're making a real effort to study—don't be ashamed to ask a counselor for help. Make it a priority, and get it done.

Auntie Says

• • •

Keep it movin'.
It's good for your
body and your mind.

• • •

*E*xercise is more important than you might think for the proper operation of all the systems in your body. It's also quite helpful for your mental health.

Even 30 minutes can make a significant difference in how you feel both physically and mentally. Physical activity helps both your body and your brain work better so you feel better.

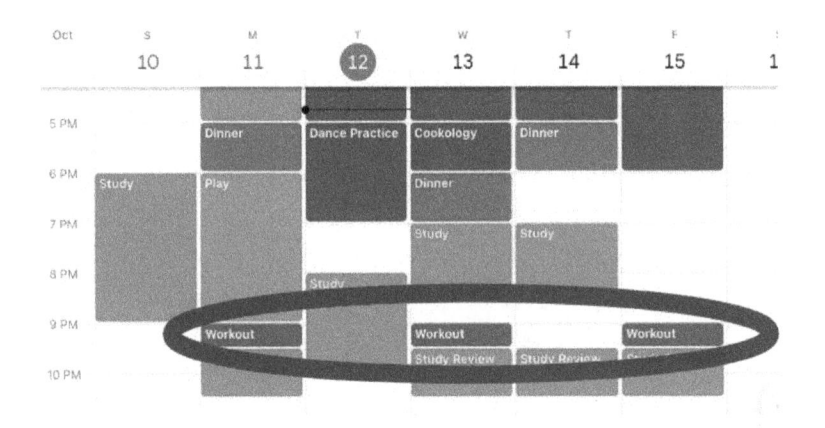

A few more things:

1. Hydrate, hydrate, hydrate—before and after workouts and all day, drink more water than any other beverage.

2. Don't trade every opportunity for pickup ball or a quick run to spend hours gaming every day. Find a balance.

3. If you don't want to work out at the gym, at least get in some exercise first thing in the morning before you do anything else. If a quick workout is a requirement before you leave the house, you'll be more likely to stick to it.

Security

Auntie Says

• • •

Be low-key
about your stuff.

• • •

Don't let everyone know about everything of value that you have. Especially don't tell anyone where you keep your cash, if you have any. Some people just use that information to steal from you. Sometimes they're the people you think are your friends, so you're not on guard with them. Maybe you're trying to be cool and not make it awkward, and then you share too much information. The safest thing is to not share any details. Why do they need to know anyway?

Auntie Says

. . .

Be ready to

defend yourself.

. . .

This one is going to be a little awkward, but if you don't know how to defend yourself, consider taking a self-defense class.

I get that your ego might make you feel like you should never admit you can't fight. It may also tell you that you would be able to hold your own if you had to. Let's not find that out the hard way, okay?

You don't know what may happen or when. A brawl may break out as you're leaving a club or football game. Some guy may try to attack you and your girlfriend in a parking lot. I want you to be ready to defend your personal space if the need arises. I'm not telling you to take over the situation and be the unarmed ninja-like hero. I'm just encouraging you to be prepared to keep yourself safe.

Bonus: the self-defense class will likely be full of single women you can introduce yourself to.

Friends and Relationships

Auntie Says

• • •

Know that not everyone is your friend.

• • •

When we recognize people because we're used to seeing them or have been introduced to them, we often say we "know" them. However, it takes effort, honesty, and time to really know someone. With that distinction, you may not "know" a lot of the people you interact with each day.

Building on that, if "knowing" someone is required to call them your friend, you may not have as many friends as you think you do—and that's okay. It may sound good, but you don't need dozens of friends.

If you make it to 21 with one or two close, real friends, you're doing great. Enjoy the people you hang out with, but understand that not everyone can be counted on to behave like a real friend, especially when it gets tough.

Auntie Says

• • •

Know who your
real friends are.

• • •

How do you know who your real friends are?

Real friends:

- are the people you can count on to help when you need something and they can't get anything in return.

- want you to make the choices that are right for you even if they're not the right choices for them.

- try to keep you out of trouble, especially with the things that matter most to you.

- will celebrate with you and, if necessary, struggle with you or sacrifice for you.

- listen without condemning or talking down to you.

- let you know when you're wrong as well as when you're right.

- hype you up instead of tearing you down or embarrassing you.

- don't make you do all the work or spend all the money for y'all to have a good time.

- are not constantly borrowing your stuff without returning it, while never having something you can borrow (this is especially true with money).

- don't sit by and watch you fail without giving you a heads-up or trying to help you work through your problem (this applies to academics, relationships, finances, etc.).

- check you when what you're doing is bad for you, even if it's the new woman in your life. If they can build a solid case for why she's bad for you, you should definitely listen.

Make sure you know the difference between your real friends and everyone else. You want your actions and expectations to line up accordingly so you're not left hangin'.

Auntie Says

• • •

Relationships are not just about you.

• • •

People and the relationships you enter into with them do not exist just to please you.

If you're like most guys your age, when you see a woman, you think about what looks good to you and what you can get from her. From sex to a decent meal to respect from your buddies, you may find yourself thinking about women only in terms of how they can benefit you. That's a little kid move. Kids often only engage when they get something out of it. You're too old for that.

At a minimum, relationships should be mutually beneficial. That means both of you should be getting something out of the deal that each of you values. When you choose and create relationships based only on what serves you, you end up with shallow connections that may not be strong enough for you to stand on when you need them.

Auntie Says

• • •

Don't be a wolf in sheep's clothing.

• • •

Don't be that guy most moms warn their daughters about. Do not act sweet and into her—entertaining conversations and activities that move toward establishing a relationship—if all you want to do is hook up. That's not game; that's lying.

Once you get to know her a little bit (see the "Try Talking without Sex" section) and find out that she's looking for a relationship you don't want, be gentle but honest with her, and then move on.

Should you be proud of scheming and lying anyway? Well, would you pat the man on the back who tricked your baby sister into giving it up? Then don't be that guy.

Auntie Says

• • •

Presenting the best
you still means presenting
the real you.

• • •

Being on your best behavior when you're trying to create a connection with someone makes sense. But don't draw them into falling for someone that's not the real you.

You've seen this in hundreds of movies—the guy fakes everything, acting like a person who might be completely opposite of him, and by the end of the movie she's in love with him—but it's not the real him. In truth, he's miserable, and the only reason it works out is because it's a movie, not real life. In real life, it takes honesty, communication, and work over time to build and maintain a strong relationship.

Strive to be the person with the habits you want to have all the time. Look your best, use your manners, pull out chairs, and open doors. Share your interests and sense of humor. Ask questions, and don't just talk about yourself. These are all things you do when you're giving the best you've got. But aren't they things you know you should do all the time? Be that guy. Do that. If she's not into you, move on until you find the person who's right for you.

Auntie Says

• • •

Be a gentleman.
Keep the details
of your romantic
relationships, especially the
physical stuff, to yourself.

• • •

Don't share every detail of what happens in your relationships with your "friends." It's tacky, and some people will use that information to get between you and your girl.

Sometimes you share because it's interesting or even because you have questions.

> This sounds nerdy, but it works. If you want advice on something, research it. You would be surprised how much useful information you can learn about relationships, about women, and even about yourself if you take some time to do some research. Read books, articles, and blog posts. Watch a few YouTube videos or listen to a couple podcasts. And vary your sources. Don't take all your information from one voice. Each person has a limited perspective, so check out some others as well.

Sometimes you share because you want to brag a little.

> That's a human thing, but I'm sure you can understand how immature and unnecessary it is. It's also unfair. The person you were with didn't sign up to have their actions disclosed and discussed by you and your friends, so don't.

Be selective and sparing with the details. Be careful who you choose to share them with.

Auntie Says

• • •

If you're destructive while
you're angry, you
need space and help.

• • •

While there is no guarantee that you will progress from punching walls or throwing things to hitting someone, if you find yourself angry enough to hit something or someone, remove yourself from the situation immediately.

You may need help learning to process your anger and emotions. If so, you need a therapist, not your girlfriend or partner, to learn those lessons. If you care for her and want to be able to have a healthy relationship, you will seek counseling right away.

Also, be ready for her to leave the relationship. Yes, you may apologize and mean it, but she has no guarantee you'll be able to keep that promise. As an adult, she is responsible for keeping herself safe. If she decides to leave, do not try to stop her. You do not want to do or say something you will regret and cannot take back.

If you're experiencing rage or severe anger, go to www.safehorizon.org or call 800.621.4673.

Auntie Says

• • •

When you're angry
enough to hit her, don't.

• • •

Being in a relationship with someone does not give you the right to hit them, no matter how angry you are. You must exercise control over yourself and your emotions. When you feel yourself becoming angry enough to put your hands on someone, leave. Just walk away.

Once both of you have had a chance to calm down and put things into perspective, you can return to having a productive discussion to resolve the issue(s). Until then, yelling at one another and being tempted to commit assault will only make things worse.

Do not become the aggressor that contributes to changing your relationship to an environment of violence.

Quick reality check: think back to the last three times you were really angry. If your anger was on the brink of becoming violent, do something about it before it gets away from you. Get some counseling or anger management classes to keep yourself in check.

If you're experiencing rage or severe anger, go to www.safehorizon.org or call 800.621.4673.

Auntie Says

• • •

If you do put your
hands on her,
leave and get help.

• • •

Do not hit her, push her, shake her, slam her against a wall, or throw things at her. Do nothing that can or does cause her physical harm.

Absolutely no level of anger is an excuse to commit physical assault.

If you do any of these things to her:

If you are violent, go to www.thehotline.org or call 800.799.7233 or text "START" to 88788.

1. **Be prepared for her to leave the relationship immediately,** even if you apologize 100 times, and she believes you're sorry and that you love her. You cannot expect her to stay. I believe she should not stay because she has to keep herself safe.

2. **Be prepared to face legal consequences** because physical assault is a crime. She may press charges against you even if she still cares for you because you broke the law and hurt her. Take responsibility for your actions, and endure the consequences.

3. **Be prepared to get help.** Even if you don't have court-ordered therapy, it is not normal or healthy to physically assault someone when you're angry. Counseling, therapy, and training can help you heal and overcome this unhealthy, unsafe behavior. Get help.

Auntie Says

• • •

Recognize and do something about verbal abuse, whether you're giving or receiving it.

• • •

We are all guilty of responding in anger and aggravation—not giving one another enough grace. On your best days, you can see that's not who you want to be.

Check yourself in regular communication with your significant other or friend(s).

- Are the things you say critical of their appearance, their thoughts, or the way they do things?
- Are you often telling them that no one else will want them but you?
- Do you often make fun of them, but deep down you really mean it?
- Do you call her ugly names that demean her (e.g., b@#$%)?

If you are giving or receiving verbal abuse, go to www.thehotline.org call 800.799.7233, or text "START" to 88788.

If you engage regularly in any of these behaviors, you meet the definition of a verbal abuser. Verbal abuse involves using words to name-call, bully, intimidate, or control another person.[18] These words can be yelled in anger or said in a normal speaking voice. The abuse can also involve remaining silent around an individual for the purpose of controlling their behavior.

Stop it.

Find a way to communicate your feelings that does not mentally harm or distress someone else. Get counseling if you need it to support your progress.

On the other hand, if you find that your significant other or friend(s) talks bad to you or about you, communicate your need for them to speak differently to you. If change doesn't happen, disconnect from the relationship, and find someone who will appreciate you for who you are and what you bring to the relationship.

Social Media

Auntie Says

• • •

Don't post
your ridiculousness.

• • •

Your friends may think it's fun and funny to post the foolishness y'all engage in. Don't do it.

You may be tempted to spew a stream of f-bombs and ugliness at your ex via social media. You might say something about the guy you want to have an old-fashioned meet-me-after-school fight with or someone who irritates you the most. Don't do it.

There are times when we have all made poor choices that (thankfully) we mature enough to regret later. The last thing you need is to enlarge and extend the consequences of such bad decisions.

Focus that energy on making better choices.

Auntie Says

• • •

Your social media
can cost you money.
Be careful how you use it.

• • •

According to a recent CareerBuilder study, an average of 70 percent of employers use social media to screen candidates before offering them a position. Over half of them did not pursue hiring a candidate because of what they had on their social media sites.[19] Even the admissions staff for some schools and programs screen social media and may choose to deny you acceptance because of it.

You may feel like it's none of their business. You may feel like they should know the difference between how people are at work or school and how they are when they're not. But that's not how the world works.

Three things:

1. What you put out there is fair game for everyone.

2. What you do with your friends is an indication of who you really are and how you'll behave at work or school (potential shenanigans, good or poor decision-making skills, etc.).

3. The Internet is forever!

Auntie Says

• • •

Nothing digital is
ever really deleted.

• • •

Do not think that anything is permanently deleted when you delete it. It is not.

Once posts are released, anyone can capture your content and do whatever they want with it. You have absolutely no control.

Remember that, and be careful about what you post. Watch what you're doing and saying while people can record you.

Auntie Says

• • •

Classes have time limits. Your use of social media and gaming should too.

• • •

We've all been there. You go to check out one YouTube and end up watching 10. You can lose an entire day gaming when you intended to only play until lunch. You don't have that kind of time to lose. You have an education to get and a whole life to build and live.

Add these activities to your schedule, or set an alarm when you decide to take a break and be social or get in some gaming. You'll keep yourself from finding out the hard way that Auntie was right about this one.

Worship and Family

Auntie Says

• • •

Don't let your freedom
hold you back.

• • •

You are probably very aware that you have the option to not go to church every Sunday. With all the options you have for how to spend your Sunday mornings (e.g., laundry, sleep, studying, etc.), it's very easy to skip church week after week.

I strongly encourage you to attend every week because while you're skipping, you limit the opportunity to:

- feel God's love in the fellowship of believers.

- continue learning and strengthening your faith.

- have people in your life who can provide additional accountability to the truths your best self has chosen to hold as your convictions.

If not weekly, I caution you to maintain a minimum standard. Decide that you will attend the first and third Sundays of the month. Or go every Sunday except the fifth Sunday of the month until the desire to skip starts to die down.

Auntie Says

• • •

You're probably going to miss your family. Do something about it.

• • •

You may not expect it, but when you go away to college, you will likely miss your family. That's perfectly normal, especially during your freshman year. Don't act like it's not happening. Just call or video chat them. When you're homesick, very few things will make you feel better than reaching out to your family.

It can help to have something to share with a family member(s). You can use it to have a distracted connection. In other words, it will allow you to spend time connecting with them while not focusing on missing them.

Some of the best distracted connection opportunities are discussions about shows or movies you both watch. It might be about food you're forced to choose from in the cafeteria, your experiences with your roommates, getting caught up on what's happening with your siblings or the neighbors, and so on.

Also, find out about your next opportunity to see them. Will it be family weekend at the college? Will you be going home for a weekend soon after the semester starts? Is it Thanksgiving or Christmas?

When you do get to be in the same space with your people, spend quality time enjoying them. Maybe you can watch a movie, play a sport together, eat at your favorite spot, cook something together, or fix something around the house. Whatever you do, don't spend all your time out with your friends or on your phone.

Hang in there. Your homesickness will lessen as you close in on your sophomore year.

Auntie Says

• • •

If you're not homesick, don't forget about family.

• • •

It may be hard to stay in touch at the level your parents and family expect, but don't fall completely off the face of the earth.

Even if you have to add them to your schedule, reach out to your closest people at least once a week or so. You can use text messages, emails, social media, and quick calls before you go to class. Call them about 10 minutes before class starts so you have a good reason to end the call quickly.

Yes, you're busy at school, but you do still love them. And you definitely still want someone to send you money, buy you cool Christmas presents, and share passwords for all the streaming services.

The Blessing

I think that's enough for now. There are probably 50 other things I could talk about, but I wanted to focus on information that would be most useful to you.

If I didn't cover something that's an issue for you and you can't apply what's here, please take a deep breath and reach out to the most mature person you trust, or give me a shout (auntie@myauntiesays.com, IG: @myauntiesays).

I pray that the things I have shared in this little book will be helpful. And I pray that you will not just survive your time in college but will thrive both academically and personally.

God bless!

Love,

Auntie

Acknowledgments

Not much time has passed since my first book was published. It was the Niece version of this Nephew volume. I am still squarely in the new author phase, so it should come as no surprise that my acknowledgements are pretty much the same. I will make a few revisions, though, so here goes.

My first and deepest gratitude goes to God. I thank Him for loving me, saving me, and allowing me to be a vessel for Him.

I'm extremely grateful to my husband for always being incredibly supportive of my endeavors. You have my unending devotion and thanks, MD. Love, DRHDW.

Big thanks to the people I thanked in the first book and to each and every person who has come out in full support of my writing gift and journey. I cannot express to you what your belief in me, expressed in words and deeds, means to me. It's one thing to assume that people support you but quite another to have real proof. Thank you, thank you, thank you.

And, thank you to you. By purchasing this book for yourself or someone else, you have stepped out in faith with me, believing that God will use these words to make a difference. I pray that God honors our intention and blesses every "nephew" who reads this book.

Citations

1. Kristina Ackerman, "Effects of Alcohol on Your Body," American Addiction Centers, updated September 28, 2023, https://www.alcohol.org/effects/sexual-assault-college-campus/.
2. "Cannabis," Cannabis FactCheck, accessed May 10, 2024, https://www.mjfactcheck.org/school#:~:text=Marijuana%20use%2C%20especially%20among%20young,consumption%20while%20actually%20on%20campus.
3. "Cannabis," Cannabis FactCheck, accessed May 10, 2024, https://www.mjfactcheck.org/school#:~:text=Marijuana%20use%2C%20especially%20among%20young,consumption%20while%20actually%20on%20campus.
4. "Cannabis," Cannabis FactCheck, https://www.mjfactcheck.org/school#:~:text=Marijuana%20use%2C%20especially%20among%20young,consumption%20while%20actually%20on%20campus.
5. "Know the Risks of Marijuana," Substance Abuse and Mental Health Services Administration, accessed May 10, 2024, https://www.samhsa.gov/marijuana.
6. "10 Negative Weed Side Effects of Marijuana Use," Summit Malibu, accessed May 10, 2024, https://summitmalibu.com/blog/10-negative-weed-side-effects-of-marijuana-use/.
7. "An Evidence Based Review of Acute and Long-Term Effects of Cannabis Use on Executive Cognitive Functions," Journal of Addiction Medicine 5, no. 1 (2011): 1–8, https://www.ncbi.nlm.nih.gov/pmc/articles/PMC3037578/.
8. Jeremy Olson, "University of Minnesota Survey Links Regular Marijuana Use to Lower Grades," Star Tribune, February 21, 2019, https://www.startribune.com/university-of-minnesota-survey-links-marijuana-to-lower-grades/506125982/.
9. "Drug Abuse Statistics," National Center for Drug Abuse Statistics, accessed May 10, 2024, drugabusestatistics.org.
10. "What Is Excessive Alcohol Use?" Centers for Disease Control and Prevention, accessed May 10, 2024, https://www.cdc.

gov/alcohol/onlinemedia/infographics/excessive-alcohol-use.html.

11. "Alcohol's Effects on Health," National Institute on Alcohol Abuse and Alcoholism, accessed May 10, 2024, https://www.niaaa.nih.gov/publications/brochures-and-fact-sheets/understanding-dangers-of-alcohol-overdose.

12. "Getting Pregnant," May Clinic, accessed May 10, 2024, https://www.mayoclinic.org/healthy-lifestyle/getting-pregnant/expert-answers/pregnancy/faq-20058504.

13. "Is Internet Pornography Causing Sexual Dysfunctions? A Review with Clinical Reports," Behavioral Sciences 6, no. 3 (2016): 17, https://www.ncbi.nlm.nih.gov/pmc/articles/PMC5039517/.

14. "Alcohol & Other Drugs," UC San Diego, accessed May 10, 2024, https://studenthealth.ucsd.edu/resources/health-topics/alcohol-drugs/.

15. Erika W. Smith, "The Condom Broke — Now What?" Refinery 29, January 29, 2020, https://www.refinery29.com/en-us/condom-broke-what-to-do.

16. Adrian F. Ward, Kristen Duke, Ayelet Gneezy, and Maarten W. Bos, "Brain Drain: The Mere Presence of One's Own Smartphone Reduces Available Cognitive Capacity," Journal of the Association for Consumer Research 2, no. 2 (2017), https://www.journals.uchicago.edu/doi/10.1086/691462.

17. Mark C. Perna, "$100 Million in Scholarship Money Goes Unclaimed Every Year. Does It Have To?" Forbes, November 21, 2021, https://www.forbes.com/sites/markcperna/2021/11/01/100-million-in-scholarship-money-goes-unclaimed-every-year-does-it-have-to/?sh=243cc9843b6f.

18. Sherri Gordon, "What Is Verbal Abuse?" verywellmind, November 7, 2022, https://www.verywellmind.com/how-to-recognize-verbal-abuse-bullying-4154087.

19. "70% of Employers Are Snooping Candidates' Social Media Profiles," accessed May 10, 2024, https://www.careerbuilder.com/advice/social-media-survey-2017.

Milton Keynes UK
Ingram Content Group UK Ltd.
UKHW021944121124
451129UK00008B/216